Looking at the
Farm

Jane Salt • Jane Carroll

Kingfisher Books

About this book

Very young children learn facts more readily when they can join in, so this book contains specially designed activities that allow for plenty of involvement.

Some activities reinforce the fun of learning by asking children to compare pictures and spot the similarities and differences. Some activities teach essential early learning skills such as the concepts of number, shape and colour.

You can extend these activities, for example, by looking for colours on other pages. You can also help by listening enthusiastically to how children talk about the pictures, and by relating them to a child's own experience. Joining in will help children to learn and will make learning fun.

Contents

Welcome to the farm

Cock-a-doodle-doo! Is everyone awake?

Animals hiding

Can you find these animals?

hen

chick

horse

dog

pig

duck

cat

mouse

bull

barn

field

henhouse

pond

kennel

stable

Who's in the trough?

Animal babies

one foal

two calves

three lambs

four kittens

five puppies

six chicks

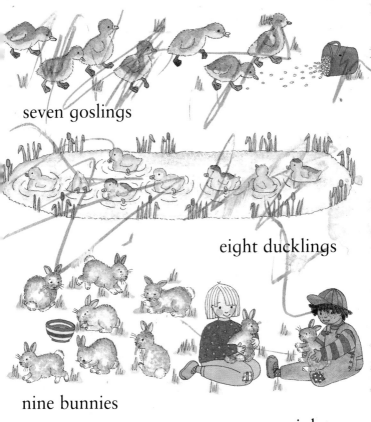

seven goslings

eight ducklings

nine bunnies

ten piglets

Pigs everywhere

In the sty,

and out of the sty.

In the orchard,

and out of the orchard.

🐔 Fruit

sweet
strawberries

juicy apples

ripe red
tomatoes

tangy pineapples

Where can we buy food?

Vegetables

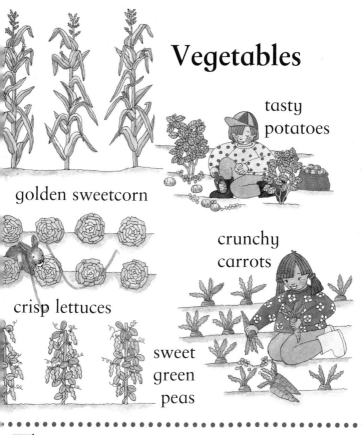

tasty potatoes

golden sweetcorn

crunchy carrots

crisp lettuces

sweet green peas

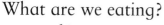

What are we eating?

Growing wheat

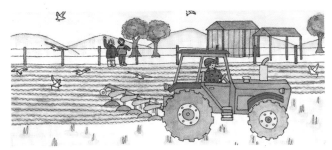

The farmer ploughs the field.

Then the farmer sows the seed.

You can
grow peas.

planting

digging

Rain and sunshine help the wheat grow.

The farmer harvests the wheat when it is ripe.

watering

picking

Animals helping

A sheepdog rounds up the sheep.

A cat catches mice.

A hen lays eggs.

An ox pulls the plough.

We are helping.

Animals playing

Pigs
loll.

Lambs
gambol.

Ducks
splash.

Kids butt.

We are playing.

The story of milk

The cows are milked twice a day.

This food is made from milk.

ice
cream

chocolate

milk

yoghurt

A tanker takes the milk to the factory.

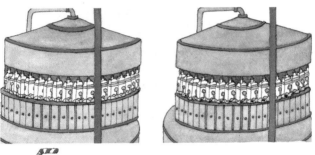

milk
shake

butter

cream

cheese

sundae

Which food do you like best?

A woolly jumper

Sheep have a woolly coat called a fleece.

The sheepshearer uses clippers to cut off the fleece.

Which of your clothes are made from wool?

The farmer sells the fleece.

The fleece is unravelled and spun, to make cloth and wool for knitting.

Hens, ducks and geese

Whose beaks are these?

It's time to feed the farm birds.
Can you see the turkey?

Whose feet are these?

Caring for animals

feeding
the chickens

milk for
the calf

cleaning
the hutch

grooming
the dog

shutting the gate

shoeing
the horse

nursing
the lamb

feeding
the cats

inspecting the cow

Summary

Here is the farm, in summer and...

Winter

...in winter. Can you see the changes?